TAMARA DUNK

These Are My Final Wishes

Outskirts Press, Inc.
Denver, Colorado

The opinions expressed in this manuscript are solely the opinions of the author and do not represent the opinions or thoughts of the publisher. The author represents and warrants that s/he either owns or has the legal right to publish all material in this book.

These Are My Final Wishes

All Rights Reserved.
Copyright © 2007 Tamara Dunkel
V2.0

Cover Photo © 2007 JupiterImages Corporation. All rights reserved - used with permission.

This book may not be reproduced, transmitted, or stored in whole or in part by any means, including graphic, electronic, or mechanical without the express written consent of the publisher except in the case of brief quotations embodied in critical articles and reviews.

Outskirts Press, Inc.
http://www.outskirtspress.com

ISBN: 978-1-4327-1275-4

Outskirts Press and the "OP" logo are trademarks belonging to Outskirts Press, Inc.

PRINTED IN THE UNITED STATES OF AMERICA

This book is dedicated to the loving memory of my mother, Bonnie M. (Dunkel) Perkins.

Had she read this book and filled it out before she died in 1982, my father, siblings, and I would have been much more comfortable with her death. We would have known just how she wanted her funeral, burial, and other details of her passing to be carried out. Instead, we planned everything in the manner we wanted it… not in the manner she may have wanted it. If only we would have known.

In the following pages you will read the "Final Wishes" of

_____
(write your name here)

Upon completion of this book, or at a later time to be determined by me, this book will be passed along to my "wish granter"

_____
(write "wish granter's" name here)

FOREWORD

No one likes talking about it, but it is something that sits out there and waits for us like dawn waits for the sunlight and dusk waits for the dark. We fear it, and tell ourselves that by not discussing it, it may somehow elude us. It will not elude us. Eventually we will all succumb to it. **It** is death.

The more openly we discuss it and talk about it to our loved ones, the better we will all handle it, now, at the time it draws near, and when its time finally arrives.

Unfortunately, or fortunately, whatever your take on it may be, we do not always know when that time is. Although we think we would like to know, usually we do not know. How ironic that when we say "**life** is full of surprises", the biggest surprise of life is usually its end. Even when we know the end is near, when a loved one dies we still feel surprised by it… unprepared… not ready. Perhaps even the one who has just died also feels surprised by it… unprepared… not ready. No one really knows what they feel. Not only is "life full of surprises", death also may be full of surprises. If being just a little more prepared for our own death or the death of a loved one makes it easier with which to cope, then would we not all want to be more prepared?

It is important to know that everyone deals with death differently. This book hopes to provide some ease to the difficulty many of us have about dealing with death and the accompanied feelings that surround it.

Did you know that public speaking is listed as the number one biggest fear among adults? In those who are presented with the opportunity to give a speech, this fear of public speaking ranks higher than fear of death itself. Did you also know that the more you prepare for that speech, the less fear you will feel about giving it? It is that way with everything we do in life. Preparation not only eases our minds about doing something, it eases the minds of others. Being prepared helps instill confidence in ourselves and in the people with whom we are about to share our actions. Would you rather ride in an airplane flown by a first-time pilot who has prepared by studying and practicing over and over or a first-time pilot who has jumped in behind the controls and decided to "just wing it"? Of course, all of us would choose the prepared pilot over the unprepared one. We would have more confidence in the prepared pilot, and it would make us feel more at ease. It is the same way with death and the decisions that surround it.

Preparation of your own death or the death of a loved one will make all of us feel more confident and at ease than "just winging it". Any decisions that can be made while still alive will help reduce the uneasiness that others close to us are sure to experience when our time comes.

Instilling confidence in the decisions our loved ones make after we pass, will help them to cope with some of the many feelings they will encounter. If we can help guide them through some of the difficult decisions that must be made following our death, it will make a portion of the process a little easier. Imagine, also, if while we are helping the people we love most cope with our death, our "Final Wishes" are being heard one last time. This book will help all of us through a very difficult time.

There are three types of people reading this book. One will have filled in the blanks in the following pages, or will be filling them in somewhere in the near future. If you are that particular person…good for you. You have taken the first steps in helping your loved ones deal with the many feelings they will encounter with your passing. Some of those feelings include sadness, anger, loneliness, confusion, and even stress. Once this book is filled out and given to the "wish granter", it will help to eliminate some of the stress, anger, and confusion that the "granter" will feel following your passing or the passing of a loved one. By relaying to them your Final Wishes, they will feel better about the many decisions that must be made following your death. Throughout my research, I have discovered that some of the lingering **negative** feelings surrounding the death of a loved one come through not knowing the Final Wishes of that loved one. By providing them with your Final Wishes you can help to ease those particular negative feelings.

Another type of person reading this book, is the one who will be reading it once the following pages are filled in. If you are that particular person…you are very fortunate. You are the "wish granter". You are the important person selected to carry out the Final Wishes of a loved one upon their passing. Obviously, the person who gave you this book trusts and respects you very much. They have listed, in the pages that follow, some of their most private thoughts and wishes. They trust that you will keep those thoughts and wishes private until the time is right for each to be shared, or kept forever private, whichever they have chosen for themselves. That information will be revealed within the pages of this book by the person who gave it to you. They also believe that you will do the best you can to follow through with granting their Final Wishes for them. They have chosen to make your journey following their death, although still not easy, an easier one. If they have given you this book, filled out, it is my suspicion that they have, throughout your lifetime, always tried to comfort you in times of need. Again, they have done the same by guiding you through a few of the difficult decisions to be made upon their passing. You are very fortunate to have someone that cares about you that much.

The third type of person reading this book, is the one who has purchased it for, and is about to give it to someone they love dearly. If you are that particular person… way to go. You are helping the person to whom you will be giving this book prepare themselves and the loved ones around them for their death. You may or may not be the person they will select as their "wish granter", but you have helped them take a step toward assuring some people close to them are provided with some of the answers for which they will be searching. They will thank you for that, if only in their thoughts.

This book is not only for the aged. It can and should be a reminder to everyone that our time here is unknown. We all want to live into our later years but do not all have that luxury. Talking to our young adult children, brothers, sisters, mother, father, and grandparents about our Final Wishes should not be difficult. If your sister had a favorite song she wanted played at her funeral, would you not like to know what song it is? If your Mother would rather be cremated instead of buried, would you not want to provide that for her? All of us want to know our loved ones' Final Wishes. Giving this book to all of those close to our hearts and to ourselves can make life's final stages a bit easier to handle. Handle them with care.

Life is a gift given to us at birth. It is literally our first birthday gift. How we choose to live it becomes our gifts to ourselves. Hopefully you have chosen those gifts well. Death should not be as feared if the life we live is well-lived. When your time has come, be prepared and prepare others. Your decisions now can help facilitate that. Live happy… Die happy…

If you are the one filling out this book… read on and think about your answers before filling in the blanks. Remember, these are **your** Final Wishes, so be selfish. It is your chance to give yourself another great gift.

If you are the one reading this book after it has been filled in, read it with care and pride. You hold in your hands the guidebook to granting the Final Wishes of someone who loves you very much. Grant their wishes proudly.

MY FINAL WISHES

In the following pages you will find a guide to help you complete the "Final Wishes" pages. This book, once handed to a loved one, your "wish granter", will help to insure that your last wishes are recognized and carried out. You will give a loved one this book so that they may carry out your wishes once you have passed. They will find solace in knowing that they can help carry out your Final Wishes by reading through the important and private information you have provided to them in this short book.

This is an easy to follow, fill-in-the-blank series of questions that, hopefully, will help you relay to your loved ones just want you would like them to do once you have passed. There is a blank page for you to list anything that may have been overlooked in this helpful guide or for something especially important to you that needs to be stated. Take your time and think about your answers (wishes). If you need to skip over some and come back to them later, that is fine.

Also, please feel free to put an "X" through any section that may not be part of your specific Final Wishes. This is your book so write in it all you want.

SECTIONS

Section 1   Burial or Cremation
Section 2   Funeral Service and Showing
Section 3   Insurance and Financial Leftovers
Section 4   Obituary
Section 5   Personal Wishes and Thoughts
Section 6   Presenting Your Final Wishes To Your Wish Granter
Section 7   Final Wishes Party
Section 8   Do Not Fear the End…Embrace It
Section 9   Leftovers and Overflow

BURIAL OR CREMATION

"X" your wishes and/or fill in the blanks.

I wish to:
    be buried _____
    be cremated _____
    donate parts to science, bury the rest _____
    donate parts to science, cremate the rest _____
    donate all to science _____
    other _____

I wish my casket was:
    a plain wooden box _____
    a nice one _____
    a specific color _____
    other _____

I wish my ashes to:
    be spread where **you** want them spread _____
    kept in an urn _____
    separated out to people who want them _____
    spread in a specific place(s) _____
    _____
other _____

I wish to be buried:
    in specific clothing _____
    _____
    in specific shoes _____
    with my hair styled by (list stylist)_____
    _____
    with my nails manicured/painted _____
    other _____

I wish to be buried:
    in this city _____
    in this cemetery_____
    next to this person_____
    other _____

I wish my headstone would read this:

_____

THESE ARE MY FINAL WISHES

_____
_____
_____
_____
_____
_____
_____

More "headstone" on page **I** (37): yes_____ no_____

Other things I wish for my burial or cremation:

_____
_____
_____
_____
_____
_____
_____
_____
_____
_____
_____
_____
_____
_____
_____
_____

FUNERAL SERVICE AND SHOWING

"X" your wishes and/or fill in the blanks.

I wish the service would be:
    held in this church/Temple _____
    led by this priest/chaplain/rabbi _____
    at this location _____
    no service at all _____

I wish the service would be:
    upbeat _____
    somber _____
    low key _____
    party atmosphere _____
    other _____

TAMARA DUNKEL

I wish these people would read/speak at the service or funeral:

_____
_____
_____
_____
_____
_____

I wish the service would include:
    this song(s) _____
_____
    this prayer(s) _____
_____
    this reading(s) _____
_____
    these flowers _____
    other _____

I wish the showing would:
    be with a closed casket _____
    be with an open casket _____
    be held at this funeral home _____
_____
    be held at this location _____

THESE ARE MY FINAL WISHES

include this reading(s) _____

include this poem (s) _____

include this music _____

other _____
no showing _____

Other wishes I have for my funeral and/or services:

_____
_____
_____
_____
_____
_____
_____
_____
_____
_____
_____
_____
_____

INSURANCE AND FINANCIAL LEFTOVERS

"X" your wishes and/or fill in the blanks.

My Life insurance policy is:
   with this attorney _____
   with this insurance company _____
_____
   in this location _____
   other _____

My will is:
   with this attorney _____
   in this location _____
   other _____

TAMARA DUNKEL

My stocks, bonds, etc. are:
    with this financial institution: _____
        agent _____
        phone _____

    also this one: _____
        agent _____
        phone _____

    also this one: _____
        agent _____
        phone _____

More "agents" listed on page **II** (38): yes_____no_____

My bank(s):
    is _____
    has money in checking: yes _____no _____
    has money in savings: yes _____no _____
    other _____
    other _____

    also this bank _____
    accounts include _____
_____

… THESE ARE MY FINAL WISHES …

also this bank _____
accounts include _____
_____

Other bank(s) info:

_____

_____

_____

OBITUARY

"X" your wishes and/or fill in the blanks.

I wish my obituary:
   were placed in this paper(s) _____
_____
   would be written by_____
   would read like this:_____
_____
_____
_____
_____
_____
_____
_____

More "obituary" on page **III** (39): yes _____ no _____

PERSONAL WISHES AND THOUGHTS

"X" your wishes and/or fill in the blanks.

I have:
   no regrets in my life _____
   the following regrets _____
_____
_____
_____
_____
_____
_____
_____
_____
_____

More "regrets" listed on page **IV** (40): yes_____no _____

THESE ARE MY FINAL WISHES

Please:
    keep my regrets to yourself _____
    share this regret with this person

    _____
    _____
    _____
    _____

    share this regret with this person

    _____
    _____
    _____
    _____

More "regrets/people" on page **V** (41): yes _____ no _____

    I wish for forgiveness from:
this person _____
for this reason _____
_____

they will know why _____

this person _____
for this reason _____
_____

they will know why _____

More people from whom I wish for forgiveness listed on page **VI** (42): yes_____ no_____

If I had it to do all over again, I would:

_____
_____
_____
_____
_____
_____
_____
_____
_____
_____
_____
_____
_____
_____
_____
_____
_____
_____
_____
_____

More on page **VII** (43): yes _____ no _____

THESE ARE MY FINAL WISHES

Here is a message/letter for:
   this person _____
   Message/letter_____

_____
_____
_____
_____
_____
_____
_____
_____
_____
_____
_____
_____
_____
_____
_____
_____
_____
_____
_____
_____
_____
_____
_____
_____

Tamara Dunkel

this person _____
Message/letter _____

_____
_____
_____
_____
_____
_____
_____
_____
_____
_____
_____
_____
_____
_____
_____
_____
_____
_____
_____
_____
_____
_____
_____
_____

More on page **VIII** (44, 45): yes _____ no _____

THESE ARE MY FINAL WISHES

I have written a goodbye letter below:

_____
_____
_____
_____
_____
_____
_____
_____
_____
_____
_____
_____
_____
_____
_____
_____
_____
_____
_____
_____
_____
_____
_____
_____
_____

More on page **IX** (46): yes_____ no _____

PRESENTING YOUR FINAL WISHES TO YOUR WISH GRANTER

Now that you have taken the steps of placing an "X" in the right places and filling in the blanks of your "Final Wishes", what's next? How do you present this book to your loved ones? Read on. It is easier to do than you might think.

Some family members may feel somewhat uncomfortable talking about your passing, while some may be perfectly comfortable. Whichever the reaction, do not think one reaction is right and one is wrong. Remember, everyone is different. This means every reaction will be different in some way or another. Neither reaction is wrong.

I suggest you select the person or people to whom you will be intrusting this book be the same person who will most likely handle the details of your passing. This might be your husband, wife, significant other, sister(s), brother(s), oldest child, or even your closest friend(s). Whoever it is, by giving them this book with all of the information filled in, they will know that you are taking huge steps in helping them to deal with and cope with the tough decisions to be made following your passing. At the same time, they will realize they can help you have some, or all, of your "Final Wishes" granted after you pass. It will make them feel good.

There are several different ways to approach giving your "Final Wishes" to your "Wish Granter".

The first is a simple and private dinner. Invite your wish granter out for a nice dinner. It may be even better to invite them to your home for dinner. This may prove to be a more comfortable atmosphere for both of you. A comforting glass of wine adds a nice touch, but if you or your invited guest do not drink wine, a nice appetizer helps give the guest the idea that what you have to share with them is important to you, and you want them to take it seriously.

Remember that you are not trying to make this a sad, somber evening. Keep the atmosphere upbeat and happy. Upbeat music in the background might be a nice touch. Smiling while you present your book to them is a must. You

THESE ARE MY FINAL WISHES

do not want them to think you have been diagnosed to pass away tomorrow. This is just something to help them when the time does come.

Wrap the book in special wrapping paper. This will help them know that it is a gift to them, and at the same time it will remind you that you are doing something special for someone whom you care about.

When you find the right time during the meal or evening, hand the gift to them. Have them open it in front of you. Make them turn through the pages with you there in case they have any questions. Maybe your handwriting needs some deciphering, and you will be there to decipher it.

Before you send your "granter" on his/her way, make sure both of you discuss who will hold on to the book and where it will be kept. Are you going to keep it in your safe deposit box at the bank? Is your "granter" going to keep it in his/her closet in a fire proof case? Where will it be stored until the day comes that they will need to open it to help guide them through the difficult process? Make a plan.

Another option for presenting it is to make your "Final Wishes" book a birthday or holiday gift to your chosen "wish granter". Having it completely filled out and wrapped in appropriate wrapping paper will make it one of the most precious gifts they will have ever received. Without a doubt it will, one day, be helpful and comforting at the same time.

The best way to look at it is to think how it would have made **you** feel if you would have received this book with your loved one's wishes in it before they had died. If you would have known some of the information that is included in this book, it would have helped you to give your loved one the kind of services and other wishes that they wished for. Instead, you had to guess what they wanted. You had to try to think hard about painful wishes they may have had. You had to search long and hard for their financial information to insure that all of their assets were handled correctly. If you would have had this book, things would have been much easier for you at that very difficult time. Most importantly, your loved one's Final Wishes could have been fulfilled without guessing what they might have wished.

Whether a birthday gift, a holiday gift, or just an important person gift, this book will be a great one to give to the person whom you have chosen as your "wish granter".

FINAL WISHES PARTY

This idea may seem somewhat conflicting, but it is actually an exciting and comforting way to deliver your Final Wishes to a handful or room full of your closest friends and/or family members. By getting everyone together to celebrate your life and revealing to them your "Final Wishes", they will be thankful to have spent an evening honoring you and your wishes.

Remember, this Final Wishes book is not just for the elderly. We should all have our wishes in place no matter what age or in what condition of health we are. Therefore, all of us should be prepared and comfortable enough to throw a "Final Wishes Party".

There are a few ways you can go with this. One way is to have a fun evening party with music, dancing, drinks, food…the works. If this is the way you would choose, here are a few suggestions.

Make it festive. Celebrate life and living while preparing yourself and your closest friends and family members for something that will happen later in life (your death) at the same time.

Select someone to be your "Wish Granter". Once everyone has arrived at the party have them gather around for an introduction of what the party is about (to celebrate life), why you are having the party (to announce your wish granter and give her/him your Final Wishes Book), why they were invited (they are important to you), and what the Final Wishes Book is about (presenting your wishes upon your passing to help ease some of the pain, confusion, and responsibilities that will arise). Make sure, after making these announcements and any other messages that you would like to relay, you quickly let everyone know that it is now time to celebrate life. Do not make the party a downer. Have fun, and let your loved ones know that it is important to you that they have fun, too.

You only live once, and if you do it right, once is all you need.

Another type of "Final Wishes Party" may be more closely

THESE ARE MY FINAL WISHES

related to the old "Tupperware" parties or a wedding/baby shower. This is more a gathering, possibly during a weekend afternoon or a weeknight. The main focus is just a few close friends and/or family members getting together to celebrate your life.

Invite them over and serve a few appetizer-type foods and a beverage. Explain to them what a "Final Wishes Party" is all about, introducing your granter, showing them the book (not necessarily what you have written in it, that is up to you), and letting them know how much they mean to you and that celebrating life is important. Allow each of them to respond or make their own comments on life, death, family, friends, or whatever they wish. Invite conversation.

Maybe have a few games prepared. To help your guests feel more comfortable about the topic of passing, come up with a game or two that can make the subject of death humorous, not scary or sad.

One of my favorite party games is the "Hidden Identity" game. This is where you write down on a small sheet of paper the name of any person in the world. It can be someone famous, someone you know, or a fictional character. Each party guest will get a different name taped on their back without seeing the name. As the party goes on, they can ask any questions they want about the person whose name is on their back, except for "what name is on their back". Eventually each guest will figure out the identity of the hidden name on their back by the answers given to them by the other guests.

In the "Final Wishes Party" version of this game, you could make each hidden identity someone who has passed away. Maybe they had a memorable death or a memorable life, or both. The important thing is to make it fun.

Again, try to make it enjoyable for everyone involved. They, and you, will appreciate it when the party ends.

One other suggested party type for your "Final Wishes Party", is to invite only family members. It can act as a kind of family reunion or just a family- building party. Do not be surprised if this party helps to strengthen the family bonds. Provoking thought and conversation helps build family relationships by creating strong, lasting, deep introspective into each others' minds and emotions. Nothing can bond a family more. The details of this party should be based on your own family's style. No one knows what they would enjoy better than you do. Make it fun.

One last idea for throwing a "Final Wishes Party" is to combine it with your significant other's party. Maybe you both are each other's "Wish Granter", so this combined party celebrates your lives together while sharing with the other guests that you have selected each other as your "Wish

Granter". This may become a larger party, but the reason for celebrating remains the same…LIFE.

As is obvious, the number of people combining their "Final Wishes Party" with yours is unlimited. Maybe your group of friends has all filled out a "Final Wishes" book and each is ready to announce their "Wish Granter". Again, although you are hosting a party to present your "Final Wishes", the book itself does not have to be opened or even looked at during this party. It is simply a time to reveal that you have planned your passing on and the wishes that surround it. You do not even **have** to announce who your "Wish Granter" is during the party. As long as she/he knows you have selected her/him before you do pass.

DO NOT FEAR THE END... EMBRACE IT

We fear that which we do not understand or of which we have no knowledge. Therefore, educate yourself. If you fear death, get yourself educated about it. The more you know about what to expect, the less fear you will have. One book I suggest is, "We Are Their Heaven", by Allison DuBois. It is easy reading, comforting, and gives a great perspective of what she believes occurs after death and how it affects the survivors they love. The author is honest, straightforward, humble, and writes in an easy-to-understand style that makes reading it enjoyable.

You can also surf the internet for books that may help you realize that crossing to the other side of life is something that we will all experience and that fearing it only makes the living part harder. Think about it for a second. If you worry about dying and hold on to a fear of dying then you are only subjecting yourself to the feelings of fear and worry. You are going to die. It is going to happen. Embrace it with calm and peace not worry and fear. It will make living that much better.

You only live once, and if you do it right, once is all you need. Who knows, maybe the afterlife is even better than life itself.

LEFTOVERS & OVERFLOW

Feel free to write in the lines below, anything you feel has been overlooked or something that is very important for you to state that was not stated earlier:

_____
_____
_____
_____
_____
_____
_____
_____
_____

THESE ARE MY FINAL WISHES

I

Headstone, continued:

II

Stocks, bonds, financial info, agents continued:

III

Obituary, continued:

_____
_____
_____
_____
_____
_____
_____
_____
_____
_____
_____
_____
_____
_____
_____
_____
_____
_____
_____
_____
_____
_____
_____
_____
_____

IV

Regrets I have, continued:

THESE ARE MY FINAL WISHES

V

Share these regrets with these people, continued:

_____
_____
_____
_____
_____
_____
_____
_____
_____
_____
_____
_____
_____
_____
_____
_____
_____
_____
_____
_____
_____
_____

VI

People from whom I wish for forgiveness, continued:

VII

If I had it to do over again, continued:

VIII

Message for this person _____
Continued:

_____
_____
_____
_____
_____
_____
_____
_____
_____
_____
_____
_____
_____
_____
_____
_____
_____
_____
_____
_____
_____
_____
_____

THESE ARE MY FINAL WISHES

Message for this person _____
Continued:

IX

Goodbye letter, continued:

CPSIA information can be obtained at www.ICGtesting.com
Printed in the USA
BVOW04s0236300416

445791BV00001B/8/P